Kiss All the Girls

by Dennis J. Gordica

AuthorHouse™
1663 Liberty Drive
Bloomington, IN 47403
www.authorhouse.com
Phone: 1 (800) 839-8640

Published by AuthorHouse 11/16/2017

ISBN: 978-1-5462-1543-1 (sc)
ISBN: 978-1-5462-1544-8 (e)

Print information available on the last page.

authorHOUSE®

Dedication

For Dad, cuz he always told me that you can't kiss all the girls, and for Deb*

Feeling Blonde

Another day
of indolent
insouciant
insipid inspirations,
idealistically integrating
interesting idiocy
into illegitimate intelligence
...feeling blonde.

First Kiss

Truth makes a heart strong,
lies break your lips,
love is a penance
served for an entire life.
A world without emotion,
empty as a political smile.
Stealing a kiss,
theft of a moment.
memory eternal,
our lips together.
A kiss stops time,
love might lead the way
when your head gets very lost;
never is a heart broken
as badly as the mind.

Hi There

Say hello to raise my spirits,
say hi just cuz you can
greet me as if you love me.
Salutations are always
accepted.
A wave takes so little to perform;
The gesture is the
magnanimity of one's heart.
Acknowledgement takes but a
moment to give,
But that look can linger a
lifetime.

Leaving Home

When one exits
the life of another,
the hollow feeling
can leave you empty
as a gutted fish.
Carrying away more
than plants—
hastily stuffed bags
full of clothing,
boxes of old magazines
(mildewed and mostly unread)
in and under arm,
and when you stop
at the curb
to look back,
to see them seeing
into you
with an emotional searching
that lets you know
they are seeing
as much into you
as you ever saw
back into them,

in a raw,
naked,
emotional way;
that the temptation
is to hold
both of your hands
over your genitals
for fear of
an embarrassing nudity
of how your most
secret feelings look
to the rest of humanity.

Twat

I learned the cruelty
of pretty young women
when pimples grew upon my face,
so I could be mocked to it
by feminine youth who knew not age
as the greatest equalizer of us all;
but the memory of a certain one
who delighted to laugh at me
—from innocence asked her out.
She pointed to her sex,
and arrogantly told me
how she could have
any one of where she
pointed at me
with what she had there.
Passing casually by,
a teacher
I shall never forget
pulled his wallet from his pocket.
Professing, in a pre-politically correct
way I still treasure:
that with what he held,
he could purchase any number
of her not-so-special twat.
Best out-of-class lesson ever!

Loss of Self

Are you alone?
Have dialled every number,
got one who did not care.
Another drink,
fuel the disgust,
rejection,
anger,
loss.
Turn in now,
go deep,
as far as one can.
What do you find?
—yourself.
Surprise
Surprise
Surprise.
Die
a little bit more
on the narcissist shore.

California Night

Everybodything go,
evil eye from hawk,
Horus makes us mad.
Everybodything go,
guts in a beak.
Warriors fighting for nothing,
Pictures, art, sound, light.
How the stars light the night.
Ningishida give me breath.
Functional schizophrenic.
Dance with my angels,
speak with my gods,
play with my devils,
bring down the moon.
—Real simple.

1/24/16

Hello?

See, that's the problem with love:
it's a shot in the dark.
You can love with all of your heart
and never see it returned;
compose epic odes to it,
only for it to fall flat
in front of the one
who has stolen your breath,
your mind, and your reason,
as if they had ignored
the knock upon the door.

Name

Just once in my life
anyone, say something to me
that is sweet and tearfully sad,
to sweep the soul of my breaking heart
away to the sun-kissed peak
of a mountain called bliss;
Just once, please.
I can name the stars,
but you can't say my name
just once.
They twinkle and glisten of love,
Just.

Light from a star,
one of them
very far,
blends with another
possibly more.
Takes a world's lifetime
before
it bathes the couple
who share a table
alone
on a patio.
Warm
with wine,
comfortable
with repast;
seeing
that distant star
reflected
in each other's eyes.
Flickering,
enhanced by candle glow,
now
comes time
to kiss the girl.

For Deb Christmas Eve 2015

Sex

To have your mouth on me,
or me upon you.
How fast,
hard and painful
can we know one another
enough to be gentle?
Slow—
talk
while we make love,
be crude
and fuck.
Will we ever find each other?
Always be selfish.
Never turn it free.
Who the fuck are we?

A Pee On The Side Of The Palace One

Angels:
ya keep blowin' 'em off.
Suppose I were one.
A pee on the side of the palace one
kept saying
I love you
to you,
and you
never heard me.
An angel
who was me
said come,
offered a hand
to glory.
What would you do—
be the cynic
burned by life?
Bullshit.
Show your heart.
Do what you are made of.
Be real.

Ten Bucks

An imposing monolith,
placed carefully
to let you know
that this monument,
made by the hand of man
represents the ignorance
of the divine that
we are kept in.
The past is the future,
so we be stupid.
When I was born,
my mother
did not have ten dollars
to pay the priest
so I could be baptized;
guess I am going
To Catholic hell.
Ten dollars was food
for my mom brother and me.
Had a sister,
She wasn't Catholic,
oh my God!
Where is her soul to thee?

Mom took it as it came,
listened to Louie, Frankie,
and the Dame.
She got soul.
Fuck the church—
they got your money.
When the show is over,
you go on.
Get out.
Next performance,
starting Easter.
I fit where?
Got no ten dollars.
How profound.

for my mom

Unlove

Warmth of a lie,
comfort: be it false.
Promise me all,
gimme nothing.
Just do it
so I can hold something
more than truth.
A lie comforts better,
truth just hurts the heart.
Hurt with honesty,
lie with love,
give what you feel,
even if it be false.

Wind

Here is to the wind
on a warm spring day,
and the long-dressed woman
fighting to hold her modesty
amusingly at bay.
Now to the smile
that comes to my face
when it is a blur
of hands, long thigh, swirl of hair,
crowned with huge wide eyes
in a beautiful red red face.

The night
of the day
I chose to leave your life:
well,
you think about it.

Fuck Darwin

Bird feathers
shelter and nurture
the chicks.
Some men do the same.
Is that why man
descended from the chicken?

Heh Heh Heh

When my time is come,
bury me not
In my maker's clay.
Do not present my remains
for public display.
Please drink, talk, and say
what a coward.
Could not
to my living face
I suppose.
There were moments
that my heart
was kind,
generous,
to prove no reason.
Good man,
some may say;
low-life,
son of a bitch, bastard
others will surely gloat.
Burn my body
in the fire of hell,
some will say,

but I shall be
at the infernal door
to shake your hand
as you all show up.

I Feel Irrevocably Sad

I feel irrevocably sad today,
wanting
to sound bright
as a May spring day,
rich as gravy brown
spicy warm on roast beast.
Throwing my heart
at the wind,
listening
To her laugh in return,
signifying
loss of want,
need for nothing.
Just another day
For a broken heart to bleed.

1/25/16

Marry Me

Philosopher's stones
turn lead to gold;
Masons make better men
from the dirty earth.
Men without love
from women, man, or child
drift unrefined in life;
seeking no shores of heaven
where peace reigns supreme;
prosperity becomes a state of mind
lost to all
(themselves, especially),
until that heart shines warm.
Coldness ebbing to forgotten dreams,
and love turns lovers into gold,
gold to have and to hold.

Generation changed everything.

Storyteller

Where now to go?
Here I am lost.
My past,
my present,
even the future:
all have come to rest.
Everyone I have been
is here with me now.
There is no escape.
We are all alone.
What lie do you wish
to live with this day?
Do you choose to hide
in another's sunny way:
liar, poet, photographer,
faker of others' image?
The mirror loathes you
when you shave in it.
If you burn your image
to the ash,
what will rise of you,
of phoney you,
best of most?

God

Hey God,
this may be a prayer.
Don't know how,
never tried,
kind of tired.
How to do this?
I do not know
what to ask for
(too damn proud).
I have all I ever want,
a few things by and by.
What can you give me
that I can't get?
My own accord
seems pretty sturdy.
Can you stop stupidity,
ignorance, and hate
in your name…eh…
Listening, are you?
I guess not.
Hey God,
talking to you.
It has been a while
since this was unleashed.
I still like it.
Yes, I am evil:
God made me in the image:
bitter and sad.

Her

I told you I love you;
the world turned.
It snowed as the season
changed.
I said that I love you again;
came upon another season.
Again, I said I love you,
you acquiesced,
said that you love me.
Again, the season changed.
I believed what I said.
You replied because you could use it.
I still love you
even as the seasons change.
So shall I,
as you will.
I still love you
as I ever once and ever shall.

It's Your Turn, Stupid

Four way traffic stop,
pretty easy on the math:
red octagon on each corner,
first to stop is first to go.
Red sign does not mean hesitate,
California stop ain't here.
Raise not your finger to me,
your voice I wish not to hear.
I have seen you drive:
rolling stop is bully.
Can we count
One, two, three,
four…
It's your turn, stupid.

10:28p.m. Oct 25/15

Jenny

Hers was a common kind of perfume,
yet her memory is still strong;
the scent of her yet haunts my bedroom
As others in our lives do.
She passed away from us
long, long before the time.
Some say it is written when you are born,
and yet, ain't it a damn shame
with so much left to do?
My naked ghost haunts me:
giggling in the dark,
rumpled sheets,
pillow on the floor,
physically, she ain't here no more.
Do you ever see me
from where you are?
Hi!
I can still smell that perfume.

Maiden

As for the company
of your sweet errant lost knight,
once upon a quest for peace,
and the time again
just spent,
truly rent,
till my lips once more touch thee.
Sleep sound, princess,
until our time comes round
once more.

Lover's Wine

Hello, old lover,
I conjure your name.
Do you ever
think of me
as I do of you?
Each day, I pass by
that house of brick.
It was old when
you lived inside.
This is now my neighborhood.
The building is for sale,
soon to be torn apart.
The wooden floor
on which your bed resided
was upon where
we made love.
Are the stains we made,
you and I;
our lovers' wine
still within the wood.
The house soon
will be no more,
but lingers forever

with me;
shall you also,
Judy.

July/10/16

If ever

If ever we saw us again,
would you slap me?
Could I kiss you the way I used to?
Would you hold your body
tightly to the curves of mine,
trembling as we used to?
Might it be political and correct
where you hold your child's hand
and smile sadly at me with longing
of what was once that now is no more?

City Light

The spark of their love
was the color of a Volkswagen hubcap.
He held out his dirty-fingernailed hand,
and she took it in to her scabby claw.
Together, they went under the overpass.
While sharing works, he looked up
to see Danny Blackguard
holding his shooter up.
Bang Bang Bang,
no bullet was true of its aim:
'twas a ricochet that tore
open across the belly,
splaying his intestines across his lap,
her knee looking like an exploded cigar;
both dead at twenty-three,
holding hands:
the way it is supposed to be.

Idiot Excuse

It does not snow
in a south Alberta city.
The gentle white flakes
that fall from the sky
are an alien invasion
when they land on our vehicles,
permeate their way through
metal, fabric, and flesh,
to take over the mind
of the operator,
turn it to goo.
There is no better way
for an answer as to why
Calgary drivers
become so stupid
with each fall of snow.

Lost Love

I still think of you
when I am awake,
also
when I dream.
You are always
the one left,
as if
you waited
for all others to leave.
Be here,
in my dream,
tonight.
Hold me close,
as if
I might slip away,
and spiral off
the world's face.

Two For Her

I wish you a day of your own:
to be filled with joy
or even disappointment,
but
still a day of your own;
and,
wish as I might
that I, too,
would be part of it.
Small serenades
sung for you
by the birds and
flowers of the world,
rejoicing that you
share
yourself
with us.

From the north,
a cool breeze upon your skin;
from the east,
knowing
your family is well;

from the south,
peace within you,
and
from the west,
me,
waiting for you.

Hurt For You

If only there were a path
to lead me to your pain:
gladly would I bear it,
to take some of your strife.
My heart is upon the ground
when I feel for yours;
Any service rendered unto thee:
ask anything,
granted, it shall be.
I know
that I am not to you
what you are fearing to lose,
yet I ask of thee
if I may be
the one
to comfort you.

One

Guilt, lining all of life's silver clouds:
the price tag of pleasure.
Pieces and fragments
of a life together,
jumbled and momentarily clear,
whirling in the mind's eye.
Shining skin,
smiling a love between two
furious words
said by raging bloated faces.
Smell of lovemaking,
a soft neck,
where her jaw allowed the nearness
to snuggle in.
Breathe
the unmistakable
that could only be her.
Freshly bathed hint of femininity:
soap (perhaps jasmine),
sudden pang of loss.
Emptiness, never to be filled again
—the only one.

Ain't What it Was

Marriage ain't what it was to us.
Generation changed everything.
To have, to hold,
till death do we part:
not no more.
We want something else
till something else
Comes along.
I always look,
So do you.
Why commit
when I do not
believe
in myself,
in time
I have spent.
Why was it
with you?

Magic

They come to rekindle the magic,
to shed unashamed tears,
share a collective cheer
or groan;
sway arm in arm
with a stranger,
move closer to the cosmos
at the church of Theater.
I love what I do,
and I will send you my picture
with Elvis later.

3/18/16

Empty

I still see you naked
when I dream.
Your flesh
pink,
wreathed
in fragrant steam;
a small lower abdominal scar
smiling thin-lipped,
showing who you are.
You were the woman
who told me
I was but a boy,
and that you were a woman.
I have your scar.

Truth Sucks

I am nobody.
Searched my soul.
This is true.
Found only who I am:
that is true.
Lie to your love,
lye and pain on your heart.
Who are you to you,
and how did you start
to lie with yourself
and all around?
Where is your real,
and how feels your heart
If you can take it?
Undo and stop a lie.
Be who you are,
or else
you will die.

Fallen Angel

Black warm water,
kissed by star glitterings.
One fell from heaven,
traced an arc across the void:
then was gone in a heartbeat
as if it never were.

News

Ah...tragedy
in our own world I see.
Ever there,
bad news
is first to come.
But
for a moment
(just one,
If you please),
when music art or life
seduces you,
renders tears of joy.
Respect
for beholding,
as if your heart
had never beat;
overwhelming your senses,
leaving you empty,
desirous of that moment.
Again,
tragedy ceases
and you live.

Never fall in love
with a whore,
cuz
they will take your soul
higher
than it has ever been before;
give
you a promise of now;
steal your wallet
and how;
leave you
longing
for what the good women
can't give;
clap you up,
leave,
cold
empty street
for you to walk
looking,
always looking
for your first whore;
she ain't the one
you'll marry,
but always,
always
will she stay
with you.

Free

I took a day off
from everyone and everything;
left my phone at home,
went out swimming,
no urge to gaze at my palm.
Watched Barry Lyndon:
(what a prick!).
Desire for just one text, nil,
drove with full attention:
my vehicle was the only one
obeying signs lights and people.
Uninterrupted grocery shopping:
really picking my fruit,
not like others:
gazing in small screens,
scooping with inattention
what may later rot
due to texting.
Desire still not here at home.
My device can whistle in the dark.
My feelings of all alone heightened
for being the only one unplugged.

Suspicion

Let it go,
let it go,
you do not know
what you think
you know.
Suspicion rules your kind,
rocks the nightmare,
horrifies the sleep.
Let it go
before
it runs you over;
let it go
or you shall die.

September 4th 2015

Goodbye, Jenny,
miss your smile.
You had a mouth
wider than a mile.
Never once did you say
what you did not mean.
Crushed me to a pulp
many many times.
We were friends,
briefly lovers,
But oh, your eyes
captivate me still.
Ever shall
you live on
in my heart.

One last time, Jenny.

Woman of Taricheae

Woman of Taricheae,
how hast thou beguiled
the sons of men
who hide behind the myth
of Christ?
Dost the Revelation
of thy warmth
expose the stone
in the heart
of Mother Church
Love those of us
who knew not.

Carcassone Oct 22/06

Free Speech Ain't Social Media

Language: any tongue
used well, eloquently
is the poetry of us all,
not the overeducated
who can tell how it may fail.
Syntax, university spew
cannot do what
graffiti in toilets do.
The language of us all,
not the elite.
Speakers of the heart,
unlike the educated, speak.
Talk bold.
Write it on paper.
Fuck social media:
that is for the lost:
no soul, no path,
blogging from parents' basement home.
Experience none,
speak if you do
pretend not to be.
If you have a heart,
it may ring true.

King Tut's Cock

Harrison could not find it,
Burton's photo made it clear:
King Tut's cock was there
when he got dug up.
Fifty millimetres big,
taped up to look erect,
waiting for those in afterlife.
So while Tut waited,
and governments debated,
where did it go?
Imagine protesters
with placards:
"Save the mummy's cock!"
Back and forth over the years,
until: surprise!
There it was:
left in the sandbox
he was left in,
between his ancient legs.

What of all this?

Sea Kelp

Put on notice,
eye is seeing you,
making your soul spread.
What do you do:
confess? apologize?
Say anything you can,
tap dance in the light on you,
but can you redeem,
willingly give in?
Go to seek help.
Once help is found,
can one help himself?
Founder as a ship,
fail as a human.
Frail as all of us are,
dream of better self.

Modern Woman Child

In the heat of the summer,
I lay naked upon my bed.
A band of light
splays across my thigh:
might be moonlight,
artificial at worst.
I find it cool...
sexy, even.
If ever you would get
off of your goddam cell phone,
or stop making pooching noises
at your small useless dog,
would you find it as I do?
Oh, excuse me:
another text came in.

Not The One

Lies, deceit, and use
can erase a lot of
the past.
Move...live...smile.
Life is yours
to take,
not anything for another
that you have to fake.

Doubt

When the world turns you out
to find that which you lost,
from the very word of your heart,
where do you turn?
Run and hope to be
comforted.
Is it your word
you gave?
The body you compromised,
or the knowing
that you are wrong:
not failed,
but wrong
with the choice made,
and have to live with.
Breathe deep,
let the air clear
your thoughts.
We all err
when we fall in love,
so go forward
into the unknown;
Have no fear
of being
alone.

Island

Jone Donne said
So long ago,
"No man is an island",
but four over-muscled,
tattooed jugheads yakking
in the middle of
a crowded street is
certainly an impediment
of ebb and flow.

Whine Needing Cheese

What would a woman
give to me
—really
other than misery?
I have raised children,
left to no sympathy.
Paid bills
left behind;
done service
for their families
more than kind.
Goes without saying:
men are brutes.
History is unkind
to us penises.
Emancipation set you free,
didn't do much
for other cocks and me.
We bear your history,
all your brunt.
Hell, lady, it ain't my fault:
A woman raised me
to respect you all.
Peace, and a
new generation for us all.

No Control

There comes a storm,
thunderous it be,
makes emotions
better than teevee;
takes your feelings,
rocks the world,
gives you a jolt.
Rumbles the ground
you stand upon.
Give it to me loud,
strip me of proud.

Peace

Let us,
you and I
drink a bit.
We can have
verbal intercourse,
solve world hunger,
poverty, strife, and greed;
Yet we accomplish nothing
other than death
of sobriety.
Put us in charge.
Beer is cheaper
than the ones we keep.
For a moment, though,
the world got fed.

False Comfort

Electric fire,
keep me warm
in the night;
put all that I fear
to a safe honest right.
Comfort me from the police,
with their endless ticket books;
the television politician
with high-definition lies.
You who say you protect me,
guard me please
from the evil that you do,
protecting corporate rights,
while undermining mine.

Electric fire,
Keep me warm
In the night.

Shitty Country Song 2

After my father passed away,
my mother would frequently say,
"When are you coming home again?"
And then I would begin to lie,
say "soon, mom,
when I get some time."
I could feel her sigh,
catching my game out.
The call comes to an end,
then I know she would cry.
Some things simple:
smells of baking.
Mind conjures mother's face,
hear her heart saying,
"Son, when are you coming home again?
There is a need to see you,
your wife and those kids.
They are my life,
my love,
when are you coming home again?"
Ain't so easy, mom,
—long ways away.
"Why don't you come home,
it is home just the same,
when are you going to come home again?"

Rejection

Free my heart of its bondage,
take it from my chest,
allow me to breathe,
just set this soul free.
We as humans haunt ourselves,
taking fear of loss
to great precipitous heights,
then drop our emotions;
letting arterial blood spatter,
crying in despair
as our own shattered pump slides
down the wall before us,
where it was flung
by the callous hand of love.

...and the angel drew near
and kissed me,
and his was the kiss of death.
My body is that of a dying woman.
So take it—
I am already dead.

—Giordano

Family

At home upon this snowy eve,
leg up on a pillar;
giving it some leave,
gazing on the shadow play
from the glowing embers,
dreaming of such I remembers;
birds caught afore memory
took them down warmer way,
chatter and shriek all the
damn day.
All the bonhomie,
all the warm
from yesterday's family
is now far, far gone.

The crafted words mother spoke to me,
given by her grande-dame on to her mum
were euphemism or wit,
folklore,
witchcraft to some:
"Drop a spoon in the kitchen,
then publicly fart".
"The very same day
when a cat washes its whiskers:
from that direction
company shall come".
Words I remember
from my mom.

Hey, boys and girls,
ain't it nice to be
drunk on a Saturday afternoon?
Why can't we have a toke,
crank up the tunes!
Ya gotta guitar you can plug in?
Strum the sucker,
let's hear her hum!
Pound them hands on table top,
blow on 'monica,
let's hear her harp!
Thump that tub!
Tap those glasses!
Youse is just being
good jackasses.
Saturday, Saturday afternoon:
we got jobs,
we got kids,
our wives disapprove.
Saturday, Saturday afternoon:
made for playing,
kids grown-up, playing.
Saturday, Saturday afternoon:
day made for making sunshine,
Saturday afternoon.

Here I am in the show mode again,
waiting to see
where it takes me.
Laughing and splashing
in the warm, soft glow,
until some fuckup wakes me;
then, pointing and yelling,
scratching my head,
ignoring all else but technical;
crawling around in greasy cable
until the problem is mended.
Thanks is a word
seldom used in my direction,
expected is more of an option.
Fear and fright—
well, they don't exist in my time zone!

Ever fall for one that got no soul,
lead you on until you think you are in front,
then strip ya down
evra chance they gots;
rips ya up,
then tears ya down.
Sex is great,
but yore heart beats hard,
and never ever does ya covah.

Thanks you

- Dan and Sara for the support (emotional and nuts and bolts);
- Dylan and Skye (he is my diamond);
- Mom and Dad for everything;
- Martyn and Dave for the unconditional love;
- And all the girls: bless them, every one.

Cuz She Is The Only GIrl I Never Thought I Would Get To kiss.

Whoseit?

The author lives and works on the planet Earth, and has annoyed the general public three other times with Charon and Demeter, Fools Are Always Nice, and Small Words in Short Sentences (with pictures).